30 DAYS OF

FAITH
FUELED

DEVOTIONS

---

*Serenity and Sunshine
in Everyday Storms*

A Guided Devotional Journal by:
KERI ANN EICHBERGER

Table of Contents

Dear Reader,

These devotions poured out of the everyday tender corners of my heart. Where unavoidable weakness simmers and continually longs for rescue - evidence that God is *always* needed. Depleted places his presence is leaned into... *and the Holy Spirit speaks.* A familiar voice that awakens the roots of experiential wisdom and knowledge of God's promises *nestled deeply in my soul.* A nurtured dwelling that then sprouts forth encouragement, and shines bright hope from the overflow, *onto the pages you now hold.* And where the *hope* of fulfilling peace, purpose, and new found joy *are finally found.*

Be prepared to grow in faith along this journey...

Through the following 30 God-inspired messages *(and beyond)*, I pray that you make the *most* of this opportunity to grow your faith by *committing* **each day** to *begin* with *Him*, AND *reflecting* back **daily** to this *"devotional time prep-list:"*

1. Grab your <u>bible</u> and favorite <u>pen</u>.
2. Seek a *quiet* spot to sit with the Lord.
3. Ask God to *still* your mind and *open* your heart.
4. Read the devotion *slowly*. (Twice if you're distracted.)
5. *Thoroughly journal* your thoughts prompted by the daily guided reflections, prayers, and scriptures.
6. Close your eyes and *share the prayers on your heart* with your friend Jesus.
7. *Cling* close, *linger* in his presence, and *receive* his blessings.

And as you step forward each day, may your path be *fueled* with *faith*, opening the door wide to an enriched life of *serenity* and *sunshine* one day at a time.

Stay connected...

While I pursue traditionally publishing my first book *(in the works!)* my hope is that this resource refreshes your soul, and you share it with a friend multiplying God's encouragement and love. Stay in touch by saying *"Hi"* on social, emailing to allow me the privilege to pray for you, or subscribing to my weekly email devotional and Faith-Fueled Devotions podcast. **(www.keri-ann.com)**

Now, let's grab a cup of coffee and head over to the next page! *It's time to walk together in faith, friend!*

Blessings, Keri Ann

Lord *Jesus*,
These words are from you,
and *for you*...

Weak. It's what I feel today.

Ok... *a lot* of days.

But don't feel sorry for me. I'm not alone.

Most of us battle with our limitations to grind out the spiderweb-of-a-day ahead. *You?*

There's bottomless mouths to feed, carpools to run, schedules to untangle and iron out... and people waiting for a *"yes"* to their request. And how about your fatigued frame that can't fathom taking the jog, working in 10,000 steps around the house of chores calling your name, or just plain getting out of bed when the alarm clock says *"move."*

We need some serious strength... *AGAIN.*

Day... After day.

But, I'm too weak. And dare I say, you're not strong enough either... To go it *ALONE.*

I know this. Yet, I keep forgetting. And as certain as the sun rises with every dawn, *God* is there to remind me of my "not-enough-on-my-own-ness" each morning when the lists, plans and demands shake me from my short-lived slumber.

Here's the thing... We have to *ask* for his strength *EVERY* day. And again each hour, as we plow into roadblocks and surprises. He's there when your eyes first greet the morning, He's with you *right now,* and He has every ounce of strength to cover *all* He sees fit for your day.

Yes, you may feel too weak to tackle the struggles and giants ahead, but if you let *HIM* be your strength, you will always be strong enough to overcome *any* battle He places in your path.

_____

Reflect: Are you feeling weak? Do you need to ask God to give you *His* strength to take on what's ahead? **(Write out your thoughts.)**

_____

_____

_____

_____

_____

_____

Pray: Lord, I am drained, and I need you. Lift me up today with sturdy confidence that You will *see me through* all the things *you* would have me do. I know it is *Your power* that allows all things to be, and that even when I feel incapable, You are *always* able. Thank you for your sufficient strength that covers me, your beloved child. Amen. **(Add your own personal prayer of praise, admission, and petition for today.)**

_____

_____

_____

_____

_____

_____

_____

Seek the Word: For I can do everything through Christ, who gives me strength. (Philippians 4:13) The LORD gives strength to his people; the LORD blesses his people with peace. (Psalm 29:11) **(What speaks to you in the scripture? Note any other passages that come to mind.)**

_____

_____

_____

_____

_____

_____

_____

_____

_____

_____

_____

_____

_____

What else is on your mind today? **Let your thoughts overflow below...**

_____

_____

_____

_____

_____

_____

_____

_____

_____

_____

_____

_____

_____

_____

_____

_____

_____

_____

_____

Discouragement and overwhelm are knocking on the walls of my weary heart. Do *you* sense the unwelcome guests?

If this is you too, I'd like to remind you (and me) of something...

Child of God, nothing can separate you from God's *love* and *power - not for a second.*

This means in *every* detail, each tiny step you take, through *all* moments of confusion, frustration, loneliness, busyness, or exasperated struggle in your day... *you are being held.* His almighty power *remains* in control. *All things* He allows are used for *your good,* because His love is *constant.* I'm talking, it doesn't take an eye off one minuscule thought, reaction, glance, or misstep. CONSTANT love.

His power is *greater* than *any* power *in* you, or *against* you. And His love covers you *perfectly.*

Therefore, you can *trust* absolutely *anything* that happens and accept it as good. Therefore, you have *nothing* to fear. Therefore, you can breathe in peace *deeply* today, in His constant close loving *presence.*

He is *for* you. He's *with* you. Always, and *forever.* It's a *promise,* dear child of God.

Reflect: Is uncertainty, defeat, or disappointment looming over you? Could you use a super-sized dose of God's *power* and *love*? **(Write out your thoughts.)**

_____

_____

_____

_____

_____

_____

Pray: Lord God, I need your power and love to infuse my fight. I know you are the *all-powerful* one in control of *all things*. I know your infinite love for me and your people will transform all things to *good*. Help me hold tight to the *truth* of your *sovereignty* and *perfect love*, that fizzles my fear. Thank you for *never* leaving my side. In your *mighty* name, Amen. **(Add your own personal prayer of praise, admission, and petition for today.)**

_____

_____

_____

_____

_____

_____

Seek the Word: No power in the sky above or in the earth below— indeed, nothing in all creation will ever be able to separate us from the love of God that is revealed in Christ Jesus our Lord. (Romans 8:39) If anyone acknowledges that Jesus is the Son of God, God lives in them and they in God. And so we know and rely on the love God has for us. God is love. Whoever lives in love lives in God, and God in them. This is how love is made complete among us so that we will have confidence on the day of judgment: In this world we are like Jesus. There is no fear in love. But perfect love drives out fear. (1 John 4:15-18) **(What speaks to you in the scripture? Note any other passages that come to mind.)**

_____

_____

_____

_____

_____

_____

_____

_____

_____

_____

_____

_____

_____

_____

_____

What else is on your mind today? Let your thoughts overflow below...

_____

_____

_____

_____

_____

_____

_____

_____

_____

_____

_____

_____

_____

_____

_____

_____

_____

_____

_____

Where am I today? I'll tell you where... *All over the place.* (Typical, *ugh!*)

Surely you've said those words once or twice? When you catch yourself zipping through each packed hour of your controlled schedule striving to shave off minutes here and there in hopes of sneaking a quick breath you're nearly dying for. In this hurried mode, if I can even manage to swing a shallow inhale, it never seems sufficient to slow my heart enough to speak "rest" to my aching soul.

I begged God for intense reminders of his light this morning. To shed *peace* over my moments and bright *hope* in the luminous shadows ahead. I pleaded for his hand to grasp mine so tightly, that straying wasn't an option.

So what happened? *What's happening?* I had cried out, God as usual picked me up... And here's what happened next... I bounced. Right back into "I got this mode." *BUT*, based on my "I'm all over the place" confession... Clearly, I don't "got" this.

Do you feel me on any of this?

How can we break the cycle? That constant back-flip switch to "control mode." I so badly want to live in *unwavering* "GOD's in control" mode. Where breaths are deeper and steps are slower. Where foggy visions of joy unblur into *purpose* and beaming *blessings*. Where peace pours out in buckets into my thoughts, emotions and actions.

So what can I do? What can *you* do?

Try again.

We can be still, reset our minds, and simply... *try again.*

Maybe you need to take a giant breath in, once again, and repeat these words with me...

God, I am here.
God, I trust you.
God, I surrender everything, right now, to your control.

Sometimes calling back out to the God, who *never* left you, is just the breath you need to refresh your soul.

You may bounce again, and again. (That's a sure thing for me!) But, God will still be there. His offering of grace and peace are *limitless.* So, reach out and receive the refreshment that fills without fail... and *never runs out.*

_____

Reflect: Are you striving, but lacking peace? Is there something you're rushing ahead with while letting God's hand of control slip? **(Write out your thoughts.)**

_____
_____
_____
_____
_____
_____
_____

Pray: Lord God, I want to cling closer to you. I know *true* peace comes from surrendering *all things* to your sovereign control. When my day distracts, and I speed ahead with my own charge, lure me back to you, the *only one* who can fill me *full*. In your almighty name... Amen. **(Add your own personal prayer of praise, admission, and petition for today.)**

_____

_____

_____

_____

_____

_____

Seek the Word: My help comes from the LORD, the Maker of heaven and earth. (Psalm 121:2) I call upon the LORD, who is worthy to be praised, and I am saved from my enemies. (Psalm 18:3) Many are the plans in a person's heart, but it is the LORD's purpose that prevails. (Proverbs 19:21) **(What speaks to you in the scripture? Note any other passages that come to mind.)**

_____

_____

_____

_____

What else is on your mind today? Let your thoughts overflow below...

_____

_____

_____

_____

_____

_____

_____

_____

_____

_____

_____

_____

_____

_____

_____

_____

_____

_____

_____

"*H*ey God, it's me, 'TIRED'... again." (Insert eye roll.)

Could this be you? With a mile long list screaming "Tackle me, *or else*... You're going to fail, run out of time, miss the mark!" Yes??? ...But you just *can't.*

You're bursting at the seams to slash through those to dos and dash over the finish line of peace and accomplishment, but you got *"nada!"* The gas tank is signaling a big fat "E!" As in, you may not even have enough fumes to *crawl* your way to fuel.

The only speck of energy you can muster is to gear shift to neutral. A place where the only hope for your drained soul to get a fill-up is to be *carried* there.

Friend, if I didn't know God, I'd surely let discouragement get the best of me in these frozen withered down moments.

How about you? Are you emptied of energy, depleted of hope, or zapped of joy?

Well, did you know, God isn't just *WITH* you, but He will *rescue* you, *uphold* you, and *strengthen* you?

It's true. So if you're tired... *REST.* Stop trying to do it all. Give God a chance to shine. Give Him a chance to show you His promises are **true.**

Not that I always take my own advice. Two minutes ago, pen in hand, I sat and stared at the blank page in front of me, waiting for words of encouragement to spring forth. But, trying to fire up a brain with nothing but fumes, left me with heavy eyelids and a nodding-off neck caving to exhaustion. (Apparently I needed to rest and trust God with my to do's.) But God *did* catch my head-fall with the spark of this quick message to share before I surrendered in stillness.

And NOW I'm *off!* To let God do what *he* does best. Take care of me, and take *good* care at that.

He's got you too.

If your soul is screaming for a time-out, siesta, or retreat - *take it.*

Guess what?! **When you're *still*... he's *still* working.**

It's time for us worn-out-ones to rest and recharge. And above all else... It's time to TRUST HIM.

Reflect: Are you needing a fill up of energy, joy, or courage? Will you rest and trust God's promise that He's got you? **(Write out your thoughts.)**

_____

_____

_____

_____

_____

_____

_____

Pray: Lord God, our souls are wilted and we need you. There is so much to do, but *YOU* are ultimately in control of it all. Help us to listen to your nudges to pause and refuel on your presence and promises. You are so faithful, and we thank you for your blessings now *and* to come. Amen. **(Add your own personal prayer of praise, admission, and petition for today.)**

_____

_____

_____

_____

_____

_____

_____

Seek the Word: The LORD will fight for you; you need only to be still." (Exodus 14:14) He says, "Be still, and know that I am God; I will be exalted among the nations, I will be exalted in the earth." (Psalms 46:10) **(What speaks to you in the scripture? Note any other passages that come to mind.)**

_____

_____

_____

_____

_____

_____

What else is on your mind today? **Let your thoughts overflow below...**

_____

_____

_____

_____

_____

_____

_____

_____

_____

_____

_____

_____

_____

_____

_____

_____

_____

_____

_____

_____

What if there really was one answer to all your problems?

Guess what? I am here to tell you... *there IS.*

Remember the oldie but goodie, *"He's Got the Whole World in His Hands?"* You belted it out at Vacation Bible School at the wee age of three, but did you grow up truly *believing* its truth? And *live* with honest conviction of those bold words?

It's true. God *does* have the whole world in His mighty hands... And He *is* most definitely the answer to your *every* problem.

Listen, I forget this most days too. But let's chat it out for a sec...

What problems or struggles are swirling around you these days?

Is it something concerning your kids? Your marriage? Maybe your work, church, friends, or in-laws? Think about it with me... How about your energy, health, or emotional status?

Whatever the issue, God has the richest peace, perfect love, sufficient strength... And ALL the power to take your situation and infuse it with the *very* things to get you through all of it. He has *each* tool to lead you to resolve. Always has... *always will.*

Go to Him. Feed deeply on His words, invest your time in His people, pay closer attention to His nudges... And *TRUST* Him. He's absolutely got the whole world in His good hands, and is *always* the answer to *every* problem.

Reflect: What are you struggling with that you need resolution and answers to? Have you called and relied on *God alone* for resolution? **(Write out your thoughts.)**

_____

_____

_____

_____

_____

_____

Pray: Almighty God, You have *all things* in your good control, yet I tend to forget my daily challenges have every droplet of resolution in *You.* I come to you in stillness and openness in this moment asking for guidance, for strength, for peace, for comfort, and offering my faith in your answer, and in *your* way. Help me run to you for all things, and trust your *divine plan* and timing. Amen. **(Add your own personal prayer of praise, admission, and petition for today.)**

_____

_____

_____

_____

_____

_____

Seek The Word: I call on you, my God, for you will answer me; turn your ear to me and hear my prayer. (Psalm 17:6) When I am in distress, I call to you, because you answer me. (Psalm 86:7) **(What speaks to you in the scripture? Note any other passages that come to mind.)**

_____

_____

_____

_____

_____

_____

_____

_____

_____

_____

_____

_____

_____

_____

_____

_____

_____

_____

What else is on your mind today? **Let your thoughts overflow below...**

_____

_____

_____

_____

_____

_____

_____

_____

_____

_____

_____

_____

_____

_____

_____

_____

_____

_____

_____

Unconditional. I've heard it no less than 1000 times when referencing God's love for you and me.

But do I *really* get it? Do *you?*

I mean, do you understand this word *literally* means with-OUT condition? As in... No. Matter. What.

It's true. There's absolutely *nothing* you can do to make him unlove you - you can **not** talk him out of it. In fact, you could think anything, say anything, or do anything, and his love for you *remains* perfectly *abundant* and *flawless.*

No past sin, not the mistake you made this morning, or any future failure could make him love you *any* less.

Marinate in all of this for a minute...

Regardless of what anyone else thinks, or says... YOU are *unconditionally* LOVED by the "Greatest of All Time."

But here's what else has me overflowing with gratefulness for this mighty love. *Because* of it... We can breathe in saturating peace knowing he will always, *always* care for us. You don't have to worry about what will happen to you, anyone, or anything around you. Because he will *never* cease to be *in the midst of it all* to care sufficiently for you. That's what perfect love *is* and *does.*

So won't you rest in this with me today? You are loved, and you are 100% cared for... 24/7. God sees the big eternal picture and will take care of *everything* in your world - *no matter what.*

_____

Reflect: Do your circumstances feel a little shaky? Do you understand without a shadow of a doubt that you and *all* your surroundings are being watched out for with perfect love *through it all?* **(Write out your thoughts.)**

_____

_____

_____

_____

_____

_____

_____

Pray: Lord, You are *love*, and it is *perfect*. Help me trust your constant good care of me and every step and stone in my path today. Thank you for *never* leaving my side. Thank you for your sovereign *protective* care of all things. In your powerful name, Amen. **(Add your own personal prayer of praise, admission, and petition for today.)**

_____

_____

_____

_____

_____

_____

_____

Seek the Word: Give all your worries and cares to God, for he cares about you. (1 Peter 5:7) For God so loved the world, that he gave his only Son, that whoever believes in him should not perish but have eternal life. (John 3:16) Though the mountains be shaken and the hills be removed, yet my unfailing love for you will not be shaken nor my covenant of peace be removed," says the LORD, who has compassion on you. (Isaiah 54:10) **(What speaks to you in the scripture? Note any other passages that come to mind.)**

_____

_____

_____

_____

_____

_____

_____

_____

_____

_____

_____

_____

What else is on your mind today? Let your thoughts overflow below...

_____

_____

_____

_____

_____

_____

_____

_____

_____

_____

_____

_____

_____

_____

_____

_____

_____

_____

_____

Would you start (or restart) your day with me here? In this prayer...

Good morning Jesus...

I know you're here. *Right* beside me. I may as well pull up a chair for you, and visualize the reality of your close presence.

Thank you for showing up. I know I can *always* count on *You.*

You're constantly ready to encourage me, and meticulously guide my steps. You're eager to extend your *joy* and *peace* as I make each move.

Oh, how I need that.

When I get up from this place, will you follow me? No, wait! You've *already* been where I will go. You've seen the road, you've paved the way. But still, *you'll be there.* In front of me, behind me, and *within* me.

Walk with my people too, would you? Rather, remind them, shout to them, that you're there when their walk gets weary and they need a hand. My family, my friends, the strangers I pass, and the broken souls across the globe. I know they need you. The hurting, the scared, the lonely, the desperate... Will you shake them and wake them from any false reality that tempts with hope in *anything other than you.*

This whole world needs you more than ever. *I need you.* I know you're with us. I know you're in control. But will you *sturdy* our confidence in that truth today? When we see so much that looks "wrong" around us, will you plow into our hearts an *unshakable* belief that you will make *all things* "right?"

Infuse my being with *patience* in your grand and *perfect* plan... each passing hour of this day. And lend my soul smiles of lasting joy in the *unconditional* love you possess and provide for me, and every single one of your children.

In your most precious name, Amen.

_____

Reflect: Are you aware that God is with you *every minute of the day?* Did you know Jesus is in the *very* room you sit? Will you close your eyes and pray this prayer with me? **(Write out your thoughts.)**

_____

_____

_____

_____

_____

_____

Pray: Lord, You hear our prayers. Give us enduring patience, and alert ears to hear Your answers... and eyes unable to take our gaze off You today. In Your faithful name, Amen. **(Add your own personal prayer of praise, admission, and petition for today.)**

_____

_____

_____

_____

_____

_____

_____

Seek the Word: You will keep in perfect peace all who trust in you, all whose thoughts are fixed on you! (Isaiah 26:3) Look to the LORD and his strength; seek his face always. (Psalm 105:4) **(What speaks to you in the scripture? Note any other passages that come to mind.)**

_____

_____

_____

_____

_____

_____

_____

_____

_____

_____

_____

What else is on your mind today? **Let your thoughts overflow below...**

_____

_____

_____

_____

_____

_____

_____

_____

_____

_____

_____

_____

_____

_____

_____

_____

_____

_____

_____

_____

STRUGGLE.

Let's be honest... we are ALL struggling to some degree. Maybe a lot... maybe a little.

Is it worry? Frustration, loneliness, disappointment, sadness, or lack of purpose you feel? Maybe a collision of all the emotions???

I hate to be so blunt, but sometimes our circumstances find their way through choppier currents before they sail upon smooth waters.

Oh, but friends... blessed is the one who lets GOD into these desperate spaces of life. Where voids are deep and seemingly hopeless...
But, where God is watching, hovering, and eagerly waiting for you to take His mighty hand... RIGHT NOW ...through your very struggle.

In fact, He's been reaching out to every single one of us... *ALL along.*

Take His strong hand today. Grip it tight and walk closely with Him in His protection, comfort and guidance, through your bump in the road or deep valley.

He will lift you back up. He will smooth your path ahead.

_____

Reflect: What are you struggling with? Do you see benefit in pausing where you are, and inviting God closer? **(Write out your thoughts.)**

_____

_____

_____

_____

_____

_____

_____

Pray: Lord God, you see my struggle. I know your heart breaks for what breaks me. Come close to me today. Open my heart to the completeness of your comfort and peace. Help me trust your protection right where I am, and grow in confidence of your superior plan ahead. In the power of Jesus I pray, Amen. **(Add your own personal prayer of praise, admission, and petition for today.)**

_____

_____

_____

_____

_____

_____

Seek The Word: Trust in the LORD with all your heart and lean not on your own understanding; in all your ways submit to him, and he will make your paths straight. (Proverbs 3:5-6) **(What speaks to you in the scripture? Note any other passages that come to mind.)**

_____

_____

_____

_____

_____

_____

_____

_____

_____

_____

_____

_____

_____

_____

_____

_____

_____

_____

_____

_____

_____

_____

What else is on your mind today? **Let your thoughts overflow below...**

_____

_____

_____

_____

_____

_____

_____

_____

_____

_____

_____

_____

_____

_____

_____

_____

_____

Stuck in the monotony of life.

I found myself there one afternoon, and battled with the all-to-familiar internal grumble as text messages flew in. Pictures from my sister and parents, both from beautiful places I abruptly became aware that I'd "rather" be. Luscious green golf course views on a brilliantly colored spring day, followed by beach scenes from mom and dad on a carefree getaway in one of my favorite vacation spots.

I wanted everything I saw. Everything "else." And that was definitely not stuck in the midst of my not-so-exciting reality of house chores, two overtired toddlers, and piles of work that had been put off far too long.

How often do you wish you were somewhere else? Or doing something different? Or being entertained by life's frills and "feel goods" over... whatever it is surrounding you?

Here's the thing though... Yes, these images dreamed of and seen are pleasing, and the views may sparkle with wonder and fancy. But what meets the eye is ALWAYS fleeting. And though you think all that's flashy, and what others have is what you want, "things of the world" cannot truly satiate, satisfy, and fulfill... and so fall short of what you NEED.

Jesus is the bread of life. (TRUTH.)

As I wrestled with what I thought I "wanted" - all the enticing ideas, objects, and excursions that whispered with the allure of fulfillment - my heart awoke to God's subtle conviction... *I have all you need, and you can have it at this very moment.*

Friends, go to Him and receive the fullness you crave... That lasting wholeness found only in God's presence and the gifts of His spirit.

Things and circumstances will not last or complete any longing, but God's peace, compassion, comfort, love, mercy, and joy are offered in abundance anywhere and anytime. And THAT is all we truly need.

Reflect: What do you want right now in your life? What do you think you really need (that's lasting) in the eyes of God? **(Write out your thoughts.)**

_____

_____

_____

_____

_____

_____

Pray: Lord, I know you want a life of abundance for me, and I know it may look different than what I have in mind sometimes. Help me seek and find my fullness in you alone. Help me to desire and focus on the unlimited gifts you offer that deeply satisfy. Thank you for your continual outpouring of blessings. In your gracious name, Amen. **(Add your own personal prayer of praise, admission, and petition for today.)**

_____

_____

_____

_____

_____

_____

_____

Seek The Word: Then Jesus declared, "I am the bread of life. Whoever comes to me will never go hungry, and whoever believes in me will never be thirsty..." (John 6:35) For he satisfies the thirsty and fills the hungry with good things. (Psalm 107:9) **(What speaks to you in the scripture? Note any other passages that come to mind.)**

_____

_____

_____

_____

_____

_____

_____

_____

_____

_____

What else is on your mind today? **Let your thoughts overflow below...**

_____

_____

_____

_____

_____

_____

_____

_____

_____

_____

_____

_____

_____

_____

_____

_____

_____

_____

_____

_____

_____

I'm a BEACH GIRL. 100%. Anyone else???

And do you know my favorite thing about it? Well, besides the soothing sounds of repetitive waves gracefully falling against crystal white sand... and the wonder of the massive blue-green abyss that opens my soul to receive all the majesty the scene has to offer...

My fondest appreciation, when the clouds make way, is "the light," direct from above, that touches the surface of my skin, grazes my eyelids, and finds its way to the center of my soul. It's the overwhelming peace that the warmth stirs within me I have fallen in love with.

And isn't this how it goes with anything "light" that touches our life? Bringing forth a sense of comfort and joy that the darkness and cold attempt to smother.

GOD is that light.

And His people are that light....

When you turn your face to God's presence, open up to his word, and surround yourself with His people, your life has an almost magical way of soaking in the richness of His luminous blessings. Everything within brightens... and reflects as shimmers of radiance seeping out His overflow of love, joy, beauty and grace.

Open yourself to His light today. Let it fill up *in you*... and *out* from you... and *bless* you... and all of *those around you*...

Reflect: What area of your life could use some brightening up? How can you open your heart to God's presence, word, and light? Or to the light others are trying to share? **(Write out your thoughts.)**

_____

_____

_____

_____

_____

_____

_____

Pray: Lord in heaven, you are the light of the world. You are the light in "my" world. Help me breathe in your warm and bright presence. Thank you for offering peace and comfort in abundance every day. Open my eyes to your light and the people you shine through to lift me up. In your glorious name, Amen. **(Add your own personal prayer of praise, admission, and petition for today.)**

_____

_____

_____

_____

_____

_____

_____

Seek The Word: For once you were full of darkness, but now you have light from the Lord. So live as people of light! (Ephesians 5:8) For God, who said, "Let there be light in the darkness," has made this light shine in our hearts so we could know the glory of God that is seen in the face of Jesus Christ. (2 Corinthians 4:6) I have come into the world as light, so that whoever believes in me may not remain in darkness. (John 12:46) **(What speaks to you in the scripture? Note any other passages that come to mind.)**

_____

_____

_____

_____

_____

_____

_____

_____

_____

_____

_____

_____

_____

_____

_____

What else is on your mind today? Let your thoughts overflow below...

_____

_____

_____

_____

_____

_____

_____

_____

_____

_____

_____

_____

_____

_____

_____

_____

_____

_____

_____

_____

_____

_____

I. Am. Tired.

Boy, have I said THAT before. (Eye roll at self.) Once again, an overcrowded schedule (I allowed) led me to the latest hour of the night, only to wake in a sleepy stupor and greet my day full of commitments with a numb "how-will-I-piece-this-together-again" stare.

I've worn out my favor requests and I bet even God is over hearing my same ole grumble *(false)*. Shoot, what I really want to do right now is drop everything... and run. Escape to a peaceful place where troubles are slim and schedules are slow.

Do you "get" any of this?

Are you pinned against the wall of "I've-had-enough" or "I'm-not-sure-I-can-take-much-more?" Where you need nothing short of "supernatural intervention." *God, can you get us an order of THAT?* I mean, He can... right? I've always preached it. He can do ALL things. Philippians 4:13 says so! It's true, He cares for and CAN cover *all* weaknesses and fill *all* our gaps. But, my attitude surely isn't evidence of that this morning...

Gosh, maybe it's not my circumstances that need fixing, maybe it's my mind. A current cocktail of skewed, toxic, shaken up thoughts.

Lord... take over my mind. This world wants to bring me down. Satan is working hard to break me. That's what's going on here.

We've all been there. ...But, I won't have it. Satan doesn't win.

God WINS.

Friend, remember with me... God is stronger than anything the world can throw our way. Let's call on Him today. He can fight this battle. He can renew and transform our thoughts from defeat and weakness to strength and confidence in His power. Oh, yes, He is bigger and mightier than anything we will face. He WINS today and every day.

Reflect: What is weighing you down today? Is it possible your thoughts need an adjustment just as much as your circumstances? Are you ready to fight back at Satan by calling on the power of God? **(Write out your thoughts.)**

_____

_____

_____

_____

_____

_____

Pray: Lord, I'm tired. The world is crushing me with its heavy weight. Satan wants to win this battle over my mind, but you are stronger and I belong to *you*. God, infuse me with your mighty shield and power. Thank you for being my rescue. In your sovereign name I pray, Amen. **(Add your own personal prayer of praise, admission, and petition for today.)**

_____

_____

_____

_____

_____

_____

Seek The Word: I know what it is to be in need, and I know what it is to have plenty. I have learned the secret of being content in any and every situation, whether well fed or hungry, whether living in plenty or in want. I can do all this through him who gives me strength. (Philippians 4:12-13) **(What speaks to you in the scripture? Note any other passages that come to mind.)**

_____

_____

_____

_____

_____

_____

_____

_____

_____

_____

What else is on your mind today? Let your thoughts overflow below...

_____

_____

_____

_____

_____

_____

_____

_____

_____

_____

_____

_____

_____

_____

_____

_____

_____

_____

_____

I'll tell you what... Miserable people inspire me.

"Why," you ask? Because, they are missing something that I have *found*, and it rocks me to the core with bursting passion to find a way to guide them to the light of freedom.

You see, I've *been* "them" before. Frustrated, worried, seeing the dark side or downside of all the *"what if's"* and *unknowns*. Letting petty things get to me, passing judgement on people whose shoes I've never walked in, and hearts I've never fully *learned*.

Do you ever feel miserable? Even just a little here and there? Have you adopted a negative lens as life has thrown you for loops and tossed you in unavoidable *turmoil?*

May I humbly tell you, *you **can** change.* You **can** remove the fog of darkness. You can have *joy*, you can smile more than smirk, you can mean it, and *feel* it. And you can be... *FREE.*

The choice is yours.

FREEDOM **can** be *yours.*

I've tasted the sweetness and I want it for you. *Desperately*. But you have to DO something. You have to lean into God *like never before.*

Talk to him. *Learn* about him. *And don't let up.* Satan will not be happy with your mission, and may try to distract and discourage your walk, but *the power of God in you is stronger.*

Keep fighting to know Him. *Resist* every temptation to ease up, and little by little your load will lighten and your path will straighten...

And the peace and joy of the Holy Spirit will wash over your troubles. You will *live* in the abounding, saturating light of His *unconditional* love for you.

Reflect: Are you struggling with what's going on around you? Does *"miserable"* ever reflect, even slightly, how you feel? **(Write out your thoughts.)**

_____

_____

_____

_____

_____

_____

Pray: Lord Jesus, the world is weighing me down. I know you are there and I know *you are good*, but sometimes I allow my circumstances to wrap me up in misery. *Please forgive me.* Help me seek You like never before. *Don't let me go.* I know in *YOU* there is freedom from *all* that holds me in the shadow of sin and despair. Thank you for the *light of your love*. In your gracious name, Amen. **(Add your own personal prayer of praise, admission, and petition for today.)**

_____

_____

_____

_____

_____

_____

_____

Seek the Word: And the peace of God, which transcends all understanding, will guard your hearts and your minds in Christ Jesus. (Philippians 4:7) Now the Lord is the Spirit, and where the Spirit of the Lord is, there is freedom. (2 Corinthians 3:17) So if the Son sets you free, you will be free indeed. (John 8:36) **(What speaks to you in the scripture? Note any other passages that come to mind.)**

_____

_____

_____

_____

_____

_____

_____

_____

_____

_____

_____

What else is on your mind today? Let your thoughts overflow below...

_____

_____

_____

_____

_____

_____

_____

_____

_____

_____

_____

_____

_____

_____

_____

_____

_____

_____

_____

_____

*D*o you know what *real* peace feels like? Have you ever been fully *immersed* in its swallow?

Maybe you do... maybe you have... or maybe it's something you *desperately* long for (me!). But yet, it feels so out of reach in a life tainted with *sin*, surrendered to *busyness*, influenced by flawed people, and pressed on by *expectations* and agendas.

It's true, *the world is messy*. Our lives are too. And, the hope of *peace* gets crushed by the weight of its imperfections.

Friends, **God is peace.** The one, the only, ALL *sufficient*... peace. And, let me boldly remind you, God is still here. He *remains* unchanged, and the depth of His serenity is at our fingertips - always has been, *always will be.*

His peace will embrace you... when you embrace *Him*.

Reflect: Do you sense peace surrounding you? Do you want God's *all sufficient* peace? **(Write out your thoughts.)** After you pour out your heart below, will you pray the prayer on the next page with me...

_____

_____

_____

_____

_____

Pray: Like the wind gracefully touching and tossing the new spring leaves, Lord I want to sway and dance in step with your peaceful steady presence today... Lead me each moment in sweet dependence on your whispers and nudges. Open my eyes to the beauty and blessings painted and placed at every corner I turn... Slow my pace, fill me with grace, and when the wind blows harder and my feet falter, may I rest in the comfort of your loving embrace. ("Guided by Peace" by Keri Ann) **(Add your own personal prayer of praise, admission, and petition for today.)**

Seek The Word: I, the LORD do not change. (Malachi 3:6) Now may the Lord of peace himself give you peace at all times and in every way. The Lord be with all of you. (2 Thessalonians 3:16) **(What speaks to you in the scripture? Note any other passages that come to mind.)**

What else is on your mind today? **Let your thoughts overflow below...**

_____

_____

_____

_____

_____

_____

_____

_____

_____

_____

_____

_____

_____

_____

_____

_____

_____

_____

Do you fear falling? Maybe not literally hitting the ground with a painful punch, but how about crumbling to *failure*?

Think about it... What are you trying to accomplish, work out, or work through with your mental or physical energy these days?

And do you ever feel slightly anxious near the edge of a flop or downfall with your latest undertaking, redo of a mission, or attempt at a task?

I get this unsettling stirring in my bones sometimes. And get tripped-up by fear of failure, rejection, and all the continual dips in the road while steamroll toward a destination or goal. (Ahem, I've been stumbling with my book proposal for the longest 18 months of my life now!)

What are *you* trying to conquer that you haven't beat the battle, or that remains a steep uphill climb?

Can I give us both some advice?

Keep moving.

BUT, keep moving forward with a *tight knit* and *frequent* encounter *with our good God*. Because *HE* will firm your steps. And here's the truth that can steady and strengthen your pace with His sturdy foundation as you don't give up...

Though you may stumble, ***you will not fall.***

It won't always be simple, smooth and painless. Many times the *trip-up* will sting a bit and you'll be sure a collapse is inevitable... But don't buy into the trickery and *lies of the enemy.* If *God* is *truly* your heart's anchor, *nothing* can take you out.

_____

Reflect: As you're plowing ahead in your pursuits, goals, and *to do's,* how often are you pulling God close? **(Write out your thoughts.)**

_____

_____

_____

_____

_____

_____

_____

Pray: Lord God, Sometimes I shuffle through the day, and let go of your hand. Help me to *never* let go. You are my *rock.* With you as my constant guide, I may stumble, but will not fall. Thank you for your solid, *never failing* strength. In Your All-Powerful Name, Amen. **(Add your own personal prayer of praise, admission, and petition for today.)**

_____

_____

_____

_____

_____

_____

_____

Seek the Word: The Lord makes firm the steps of the one who delights in him; though he may stumble, he will not fall, for the Lord upholds him with his hand. (Psalm 37:23-24) **(What speaks to you in the scripture? Note any other passages that come to mind.)**

_____

_____

_____

_____

_____

_____

_____

_____

_____

_____

_____

_____

_____

_____

What else is on your mind today? Let your thoughts overflow below...

_____

_____

_____

_____

_____

_____

_____

_____

_____

_____

_____

_____

_____

_____

_____

_____

_____

_____

_____

*H*ere I am again waffling with emotions... Willing away and suppressing desires of my flesh for more comfort, ease, and security.

It's tough to return to routine life after indulging in any sort of pleasure-filled escape. Amen?!

This was me after a recent vacation. Questioning if the real world "disconnect" is even worth it. Disappointment attempts to squash us all when we step back into our "less than ideal" reality, right?

Yes, sometimes it does...*IF*. If we *choose* to let it. If we choose to listen to the enemy's temptations to face our heavy circumstances with defeat and loads of "whoa is me's."

Do you ever dread the monotonous day ahead with temptations to peer back at the sparkle and peace behind you, and move fast forward to prettier places of bliss and joy?

I've been on the verge of falling to Satan's deceptive charm too many times. I've even made the subconscious decision to cave and found myself in deeper pits of self-pity, jealousy and discontentment that steal ALL the joy and peace my soul craves.

I don't want that. And I bet you don't either. No, you want that peace back... you want the *joy* to return... and to stay... For a while.

And friends, there is only one real *way* to get there... *God's way.*

So, you can take Satan's sneaky lies and your tricky thoughts captive, toss them out, and replace them with TRUTH. The TRUTH that you can have all those delightful gifts you long for, right where you are.

God's radiant TRUTHS and promises, found in His word, that beam
with the depth of hope, the grandeur of joy, the overflowing of peace,
and endless unconditional love. Everything you desire... Everything
you need.

Reflect: What are you focusing on in the past or future that's
distracting you from what God has in front of you today? **(Write out
your thoughts.)**

Pray: Lord Jesus, you've given me such beautiful gifts and I'm guilty
of wanting more... and more. I want to be thankful for the *lot* and
thankful for the *less*. Because ALL things, ALL moments you give, are
gifts. Forgive me for letting Satan tempt me with filters of lack, and
replace them with your lens of abundance no matter what surrounds
me. You are sovereign, you are the truth, and you are so good... *ALL*
the time. In your gracious name I pray. Amen. **(Add your own
personal prayer of praise, admission, and petition for today.)**

_____

_____

_____

_____

_____

Seek The Word: We demolish arguments and every pretension that sets itself up against the knowledge of God, and we take captive every thought to make it obedient to Christ. (2 Corinthians 10:5) Jesus said to him, "I am the way, and the truth, and the life." (John 14:6) "If you look for me wholeheartedly, you will find me." (Jeremiah 29:13) **(What speaks to you in the scripture? Note any other passages that come to mind.)**

_____

_____

_____

_____

_____

_____

_____

_____

What else is on your mind today? Let your thoughts overflow below...

_____

_____

_____

_____

_____

_____

_____

_____

_____

_____

_____

_____

_____

_____

_____

_____

_____

_____

_____

Why the heavy heart this morning? I ask myself.

The horizon looks pretty bright and God's presence has felt close. But even still, a gray cloud subtly shields His joyful light.

Satan, the deceiver, knows he must work fresh angles to hold me down. Lately his sneak attacks slither in through my weariness, my busyness, and even in the vulnerability of the middle of night or my dreams. There the enemy attempts to bulldoze God's peace before I can even start my day. How clever! How cruel...

Like to admit it or not, the master con artist is working on all of us in some disguised form. Exerting relentless pursuits to drown out all comfort, joy, and sunlit perspectives.

BUT... I have the armor of God. *And so do you.*

You can fight and resist with the ultimate victor. *GOD* is stronger. *Oh so much stronger.* With unlimited power to fight any opposition that you come against. Time spent with Him, time immersed in His word, shrivels away the enemy and his progress to darken my spirit. It will do the same for you.

If you are feeling the pull to darkness, or a bit heavyhearted... open the door wide to God's light. Marinate in an abundance of His words, engage in sweet lingering conversation and praise... for all that He is, and all He is doing to tend to you, His precious beloved child.

Reflect: Do you feel darkness creeping in on you? How can you re-prioritize your plans to feed on God's light today? **(Write out your thoughts.)**

_____

_____

_____

_____

_____

_____

Pray: Dear Lord Jesus, you are the light of my life. Though the enemy strives to take that away, I know you are always near and always more powerful. Nothing can separate me from your love. Help me seek you with all that I am, so I may stand sturdy against the darkness that wills to mask your radiance. Ground me firmly in your abounding strength and delightful presence... *Amen.* **(Add your own personal prayer of praise, admission, and petition for today.)**

_____

_____

_____

_____

_____

Seek The Word: Therefore, put on every piece of God's armor so you will be able to resist the enemy in the time of evil. Then after the battle you will still be standing firm. (Ephesians 6:13) For once you were full of darkness, but now you have light from the Lord. So live as people of light! (Ephesians 5:8) **(What speaks to you in the scripture? Note any other passages that come to mind.)**

_____

_____

_____

_____

_____

_____

_____

_____

_____

_____

_____

_____

_____

_____

_____

_____

What else is on your mind today? **Let your thoughts overflow below...**

_____

_____

_____

_____

_____

_____

_____

_____

_____

_____

_____

_____

_____

_____

_____

_____

_____

_____

_____

_____

Overwhelmed? Have you ever taken on too much? *(Maybe now?)* And then you ask yourself, what can possibly go... right? *I feel the serious need for a bit more margin in my life. BUT GOD... what in the world would you possibly want me to give up?! It all looks so "good," so "serving," so for YOU. And for your people. I've made commitments... and they NEED me. Beyond that, they need the "best" of me. But my best is gone.*

Isolated from the world in the comfort of my bedroom, I allow secret tears to slip. Tears of defeat, tears of weakness, overwhelm, and uncertainty.

Sound familiar? Can you relate to these emotions?

I protest in desperation... *Lord, show me a way out. Guide me away from what needs to go, or please, send me your strength. ...I am asking for HELP.*

HELP.

Wait, is that it? Is that the *answer?*

Sometimes God *does* want us to cut some stuff out. But many times, HELP is the key. We can not do this life alone. Friend, ask God for *help.* God *wants* to help. But do not forget to ask *people* for help too.

God created us to depend on him. And many times, that looks like leaning on the people he sends our way. In fact, he's nudging someone's heart right now to serve *you.* Someone in your life's path is literally praying for a sign from God to reveal who they should serve.

Ask others for help, and let God help you *through* them.

When giving up something on your list, or schedule of commitments, doesn't seem to be the answer, *HELP* is often just what God wants to give you. Open your gracious heart, open your bold voice, open your humble ears... and open the way to God's abounding strength and compassionate help poured out *to you*.

Reflect: What can you ask God for help with today? Who can you bless by allowing them to serve you? **(Write out your thoughts.)**

_____

_____

_____

_____

_____

_____

Pray: God, Thank you for always listening to our cries and for opening the hearts of others. Help me to trust your answers and your perfect timing. In your mighty name I pray... Amen. **(Add your own personal prayer of praise, admission, and petition for today.)**

_____

_____

_____

_____

_____

_____

_____

Seek The Word: Carry each other's burdens, and in this way you will fulfill the law of Christ. (Galatians 6:2) My help comes from the LORD, the Maker of heaven and earth. (Psalm 121:2) **(What speaks to you in the scripture? Note any other passages that come to mind.)**

_____

_____

_____

_____

_____

_____

_____

_____

_____

_____

_____

_____

_____

What else is on your mind today? Let your thoughts overflow below...

_____

_____

_____

_____

_____

_____

_____

_____

_____

_____

_____

_____

_____

_____

_____

_____

_____

_____

_____

You shouldn't do it. ...Yes, you should. It's the right thing to do for him, for her... for you... or is it??? *God wants you to rest.* No, Satan is tricking you! Of course he wants you to say "no" to this, that, or *them*, and avoid producing good in this world... **Which voice do I listen to?**

It was the first day of summer and the season's abrupt transition brought on corresponding thoughts that collided into a clutter of conflict. Calm to chaos. Additional bodies crowding yesterday's empty space with a barrage of social, mental, physical and emotional needs and requests. Piled on top of exhaustion from an over committed calendar and a hurried week of crash prep for all of *this*. It's no wonder my thoughts were tossed in a whiplash of debilitating confusion. **Can you relate???**

My head fell hard on my pillow that night in defeat. But as God always hears our cries for relief, the heavens opened and rain poured down the following morning, cancelling *all things*. Ahh... exhale... I think the Big Man does this just for us "crazies" sometimes. Inclement weather to cancel activities, clearing schedules of debris and busy. In my case, allowing a necessary date night...

While venting my struggle over dinner, to hear God through all the noise, Mike released an empathetic response, full of profound truth. "Keri, I'd say if you can't discern the voice of God from Satan you probably need to *slow down*."

I released a chuckle, received an exception to break a date night rule to pull out my phone, and jotted down his wise words, to reflect on later. "You're so right." I conceded. Not much could be more true of what I was experiencing.

Friend, if you're struggling to hear God's voice, might I suggest the same for you? That you need to *slow down* a bit?

I indulged in a much needed mental health day the next day. Could I afford to? Could my work, my kids, my commitments afford my absence? I decided I couldn't afford *not* to.

We need God's direction and counsel for every choice point in our day. All throughout our life in fact. Left alone with our chaotic schedules and the expectations of others, the enemy will muffle our ears, whisper lies, and blind our spiritual sight, throwing us in the fire of confusion and complete depletion. Leaving us nothing... for *anyone*.

We have to learn to slow down, refuel, rest, inhale refreshment... and many times take even more time than we *think* we need. The enemy will tell you not to, but God wants your time. God longs to care for you and restore your soul so you can be filled *with* Him... and *for* Him.

_____

Reflect: Are you surrounded by overload and noise? Hearing only conflicting whispers, confused which instruction to follow? **(Write out your thoughts.)**

_____

_____

_____

_____

_____

_____

_____

Pray: Lord God, I want your voice to be the one that speaks loudly to my soul. I know your way is the better way, but I get so confused in the hustle and hassle. Help me put aside all things for you today, so I can slow down and listen for your sweet words of wisdom. Thank you for your peace and guidance that speaks truth over my life. In your perfect name I pray... Amen. **(Add your own personal prayer of praise, admission, and petition for today.)**

_____

_____

_____

_____

_____

_____

Seek The Word: Call to me and I will answer you, and will tell you great and hidden things that you have not known. (Jeremiah 33:3) Let all that I am wait quietly before God, for my hope is in him. (Psalm 62:5) **(What speaks to you in the scripture? Note any other passages that come to mind.)**

_____

_____

_____

_____

_____

What else is on your mind today? Let your thoughts overflow below...

_____

_____

_____

_____

_____

_____

_____

_____

_____

_____

_____

_____

_____

_____

_____

_____

_____

_____

I have so much I want to say... but sometimes don't. *Anyone?*

Thoughts, opinions, frustrations, and passions. They may simmer at the surface, and then fizzle with the next distraction. But other times, the flames blaze wild in my mind and seem *impossible* to contain.

When do I *release* the fire? When do we let loose the storming sea of perspectives? Or unleash our *words* to the world - or to *one*?

Does God want me to speak, or remain *silent*? After all, *HE* is the one to consult with whatever we allow to slip from our tempted lips.

If you've been in a similar predicament - high on passion and perspectives - can I offer some *faith-filled* advice to both of us?

How *still* have you been before deciding to spill your *heart*?

How much have you asked *God* to infuse His *wisdom* into your very thoughts?

How much *LOVE*, over anger, bitterness, pride, and judgment are you filtering your processing through? Are you feeling any of those ill feelings before you release your reproach? Or has love, unity, and the ultimate hope of *pointing your audience to Christ* consumed your intentions with genuine desire to fulfill the Great Commission?

Whatever you say, say it *out of love.*

Whatever you do, do it to bring *unity to God's people.*

Whatever you consider, consider it with the *heart of the Holy Spirit.*

If your heart is Christ-filled and pure, and you have paused and passed your thoughts by the *only one* whose opinion matters, may you carry-on in God's grace as you point people in *love* and *unity* to the *hope in HIM* this world is so desperate for.

I pray your thoughts will be *His* thoughts. I pray your words will be *His* words. I pray your *hope* is in *Him*.

_____

Reflect: Do you have opinions and perspectives perplexing you? Have you been filtering your thoughts, words, and judgments through the *heart of God* and his unconditional love for *all people*? **(Write out your thoughts.)**

_____

_____

_____

_____

_____

_____

Pray: Lord, when our passions burn with desire to share what's inside, may you pour your love, your mercy, and your grace into our hearts. So that we will be full of *your wisdom*. Help us look to you in all we do. *We love you.* Our hope is in *you*. Thank you for your faithfulness. In your mighty name, Amen. **(Add your own personal prayer of praise, admission, and petition for today.)**

_____

_____

_____

_____

_____

_____

_____

Seek the Word: Whatever you do, work at it with all your heart, as working for the Lord, not for human masters. (Colossians 3:23) So let's stop condemning each other. Decide instead to live in such a way that you will not cause another believer to stumble and fall. (Romans 14:13) So then, let us aim for harmony in the church and try to build each other up. (Romans 14:19) **(What speaks to you in the scripture? Note any other passages that come to mind.)**

_____

_____

_____

_____

_____

_____

_____

_____

What else is on your mind today? Let your thoughts overflow below...

_____

_____

_____

_____

_____

_____

_____

_____

_____

_____

_____

_____

_____

_____

_____

_____

_____

_____

*H*ave you been idle for too long? Stagnant maybe in your thoughts, your motivation, or your *inspiration*?

There's something MORE. Do you sense that?

Untapped possibility and beauty awaits you. And you want to be set free. To flee the limits of your physical space, or maybe to escape the confines of your stubborn soul.

I feel it.

Why do we become trapped? Bound by our comfort or expectations, wrapped up in the world's molds of perfection, or enclosed in self-inflicted rigidity that binds our hearts and bodies.

Oh, but I see a GREAT BIG world. I've tasted a touch of God's rich blessings, and I know there's infinitely more. *More for you too...* Boundless love to embrace, permeating joy to experience, swelling peace to revel in, and deep purpose to engulf *each* of us. Beyond what the heart can fathom and the eyes can see.

What if we pushed through the surface fluff that surrounds us, pulled back the curtain that distracts us, and ripped off the ropes that tie us down... and tapped into the *depth* of what God has written on our hearts? Beyond the limits of our sight and worldly views. Beyond our worries, fears and prideful resistance.

God indeed offers *immeasurable* blessings... through His spirit within us, His people among us, His dazzling works smothering creation, and in His grand plans for me and you.... *All* of this when we peer above the waves of the world, unleash our hearts and unshackle our feet... and step through the walls of our fickle hearts into the awe-inspiring *goodness* our mighty God has in store.

If you're feeling that sense of entrapment, that longing for more... won't you join me in grabbing a hold of God's call today? Leap out of your comfort and walk with bold obedience into the path of *His* fulfilling future designed *uniquely* for you.

Friend... There's endless blessings that await, when you walk in *obedience* toward God.

_____

Reflect: Where have you become idle in your thoughts or actions? What can you do today to take just one step closer to God? **(Write out your thoughts.)**

_____

_____

_____

_____

_____

_____

_____

Pray: Lord Jesus, You have created a beautiful world full of possibilities. Though I tend to sway to safety and overlook many of the gifts and much of the potential you offer, may you open my eyes wide that I may follow your lead into the richness you planned. Thank you for your unconditional care. In your wonderful name I pray... Amen.

(Add your own personal prayer of praise, admission, and petition for today.)

_____

_____

_____

_____

_____

_____

_____

_____

Seek The Word: See, I am setting before you today a blessing and a curse— the blessing if you obey the commands of the Lord your God that I am giving you today; the curse if you disobey the commands of the Lord your God and turn from the way that I command you today by following other gods, which you have not known. (Deuteronomy 11:26-28) All these blessings will come on you and accompany you if you obey the LORD your God. (Deuteronomy 28:2) **(What speaks to you in the scripture? Note any other passages that come to mind.)**

_____

_____

_____

_____

_____

_____

What else is on your mind today? Let your thoughts overflow
below...

_____

_____

_____

_____

_____

_____

_____

_____

_____

_____

_____

_____

_____

_____

_____

_____

_____

_____

_____

*D*o you feel like you're wasting time being *still*?

I would imagine all heads are nodding. Yes?

Hey, I get it. I'm with you. There is tons to be done, and it never stops. Like a conveyor belt with no pause button, life keeps dishing out more tasks, more decisions, more to dos, and more stuff that needs... You.

But how well can you handle the task before you without proper instruction? How effective will your decisions be without adequate wisdom? And how much room for error is there when you're wired up with tangled anxious thoughts, instead of clear smooth effective processors.

I've tried it, over and over again. To run full speed into the day fueled by fleeting fumes of my own will. It never quite cuts it.

As much as the enemy wants me to believe the world's constant chirp of "hustle harder" ...God knows better.

He knows that HE is the true source of productivity and success. Producing the only fruits that manifest His good plans and purpose.

Friends, spending time with God fills and fuels with the fruits of the Spirit. They are... love, joy, peace, patience, kindness, goodness, faithfulness, gentleness, self-control. Without them we would be counterproductive... seemingly worthless.

What do you say we rely on God's standard of success? Starting or interrupting our day, filling up on Him, so we can be restored strong IN Him, and FOR Him. *His* fruit is our true source of wisdom and strength... Without it, "ourselves" cannot be trusted.

So instead of perceiving time as "wasted" being still, know you would be wasting your precious time "striving," when you're not doing it, *filled with Him*.

_____

Reflect: Are you prioritizing time with God as essential for your productivity? Are you giving God enough of your time in order to restore your soul? **(Write out your thoughts.)**

_____

_____

_____

_____

_____

_____

_____

Pray: Lord God, You see me striving at my own hurried pace and it saddens you. How you long for me to sit with you and fill up with your love, joy, peace, patience, kindness, goodness, faithfulness, gentleness, self-control. Solidify my belief that within these things is where I will find true success. Still me today that I may become saturated with You, so I can pour out *for* you. Thank you Jesus. Amen. **(Add your own personal prayer of praise, admission, and petition for today.)**

_____

_____

_____

_____

_____

_____

_____

Seek The Word: "Yes, I am the vine; you are the branches. Those who remain in me, and I in them, will produce much fruit. For apart from me you can do nothing." (John 15:5) "But the fruit of the Spirit is love, joy, peace, patience, kindness, goodness, faithfulness, gentleness, self-control; against such things there is no law." (Galatians 5:22-23) **(What speaks to you in the scripture? Note any other passages that come to mind.)**

_____

_____

_____

_____

_____

_____

_____

_____

_____

What else is on your mind today? **Let your thoughts overflow below...**

_____

_____

_____

_____

_____

_____

_____

_____

_____

_____

_____

_____

_____

_____

_____

_____

_____

_____

_____

*D*o you ever struggle with... *YOU?* Does it seem there's just something about you that goes against the grain, gets in others' way, or inconveniences someone?

How about *this*... Do you long to slink away from crowds when your heart is *crowded?*

I sure do.

Here's a peek at my wacky conscience these days... *"If I could only be more social, exude abundant energy, speak the perfect words, acquire that magnetic charm generating ease in those around me, I could be oodles more comfortable... more happy... more of all the 'good stuff.' Oh, and people would like and approve of me more too! Then, God could REALLY use me. THEN, I'd shine as the bright light I long to be to everyone in my path."*

But life doesn't quite transpire this way. Many times, *many of us,* don't feel we fit our surroundings. Personally, I rarely feel full enough to fill the wide gaping spaces, loud enough to match the noise, energetic enough to keep the pace of the room. I wonder... How is everyone else doing it? How do they find all that *"enough-ness?"* Or do they wish to crawl into hibernation for a season too?

Should I? Should *you?* Can God *use* a soul hiding alone where no one but HE is present?

When all I want is to run from the "overwhelm," I assume that I must be missing something! I just don't have "enough" to offer my surroundings. ...But, but, b*uuuut!* Friend, this is the enemy's trickery. If you're hearing these deceptive "not enough" voices you're being deceived too. The truth is, God calls us ON purpose... God made you like YOU **on purpose**. And, it may very well be to fill you full in private in order to pour on to *others* in public.

We all need to retreat to quiet spaces where our thoughts are free to hear God clearly. Regardless of who and what "seems" in need, this is not something to feel guilt, shame, or discouragement about. Go there, run there, *stay* there a while... let God fill you up. It's part of His *perfect plan* for you... *and* for those around you.

_____

Reflect: Are you feeling like you don't measure up to your own big expectations or the pace of others? Could it be that God is luring you in for some much needed alone time with *Him*? **(Write out your thoughts.)**

_____

_____

_____

_____

_____

Pray: Dear Lord, I admit, I feel inadequate so many days, like I'm falling short of the fullness I misperceive in others. But God, help me notice in me what *you* see, a perfectly planned creation that needs *you* more than *anything*. A soul that requires a *full* filling of You to pour back out to others. Help me know that *alone with you* is exactly where you want me. On purpose, for a *great* purpose. Thank you for your *non-stop* loving presence. Amen. **(Add your own personal prayer of praise, admission, and petition for today.)**

_____

_____

_____

_____

_____

_____

Seek The Word: But when you pray, go away by yourself, shut the door behind you, and pray to your Father in private. Then your Father, who sees everything, will reward you. (Matthew 6:6) Be still, and know that I am God! I will be honored by every nation. I will be honored throughout the world. (Psalm 46:10) **(What speaks to you in the scripture? Note any other passages that come to mind.)**

_____

_____

_____

_____

_____

_____

What else is on your mind today? **Let your thoughts overflow below...**

_____

_____

_____

_____

_____

_____

_____

_____

_____

_____

_____

_____

_____

_____

_____

_____

_____

_____

_____

_____

_____

*D*o you feel *safe?* Maybe an unsettling sense of potential harm isn't your struggle - *or maybe it is* - but how about safety from emotional turmoil? Disappointment, rejection, overwhelm? Pause and think for a minute. Are any of these destructive forces surrounding you with discomfort and insecurity lately?

When we are safe and secure we feel *protected* from potential physical, mental, or emotional harm and battles.

Do you *feel protected?* I bet you'd like to lather on and adopt a *constant* sense of protection. I know I would!

I've got good news... Though we are not immune to trials and troubles, we *ARE* protected. *...Always.*

It sounds so simple. Of course, it doesn't always *FEEL* so simple, huh? Because it's true, the enemy will never stop tugging away and pulling us down. He's *relentless* to imprison every single one of us in *fear* - a dreadful space where safety and security are smothered by darkness.

No doubt, the world doesn't feel safe. Shoot, I don't always feel safe from attacks of the enemy in my own home! (Sneaky little devil!) ...But, *GOD is our protector.*

Friend, cling *close* to your *protector.* And then a little closer. Let's let *HIM* be our *fortress.*

If you'll lean hard on Him and escape under *His* wings, you can *trust* that He will *shelter* you with his peaceful presence, *shield* you with his constant comfort, and will *NEVER fail you.*

You are *always* safe with our Lord *Jesus.*

_____

Reflect: Do you feel exposed or unsettled by the fear of potential physical, mental, or emotional defeat or harm? **(Write out your thoughts.)**

_____

_____

_____

_____

_____

_____

Pray: Lord, I don't always feel so safe in this world. Fear of what might happen parades around in my mind. Help me cling to *you*. Help me sense your presence and protection, and trust your *unshakable* shelter. You are my *shield*. You are *so good*. And I thank you. In your *faithful* name, Amen. **(Add your own personal prayer of praise, admission, and petition for today.)**

_____

_____

_____

_____

_____

_____

_____

Seek the Word: In peace I will lie down and sleep, for you alone, Lord, make me dwell in safety. (Psalm 4:8) He will cover you with his feathers, and under his wings you will find refuge; his faithfulness will be your shield and rampart. (Psalm 91:4) **(What speaks to you in the scripture? Note any other passages that come to mind.)**

_____

_____

_____

_____

_____

_____

_____

_____

_____

_____

_____

_____

_____

_____

What else is on your mind today? Let your thoughts overflow below...

_____

_____

_____

_____

_____

_____

_____

_____

_____

_____

_____

_____

_____

_____

_____

_____

_____

_____

_____

God wants to give you *so* much more.

Do you believe this? I mean, the Bible says it, and I *do* believe the Bible. But, truth be told, I'm struggling to convince myself these days that it's true.

Here's the deal. I've been crazy-train working my tail off. Little potential TMI transparency here... With no pay. It actually costs me money, that I question I should be spending, to house my email list and send my weekly devotional. I LOVE what I do, but I sacrifice my family, friends, husband, housework, and loads of other serving opportunities that arise, to follow a calling I'm not always 100% sure wasn't a butt dial. (Sorry to be so crude.)

Oh, the *"what if's"* and worries that spiral into a funnel cloud over my baffled brain... Have I gotten this right? *Will it be worth it?* Is God's plan for me, *and all this*, really for good? I may impact a couple confused or thirsty souls, but is it *worth* the price I'll pay? The price that *others* who need me have to pay?

What are *you* up to lately that you wonder if it's *really* worth it?

When you grind out the **hard**, are you grinning ear to ear with joy and confidence that God has blessings waiting to shower on you for your obedience, as He promised? *(Or not?)*

Geez, I wish I could smack that truth into my weary soul with jolts of assurance and energy.

Maybe we *both* need to level-set for a minute. Reality check with me, will you? *Here it goes...*

Hey you! Hey me! Fighting the good fight, walking the rocky road. Following the lead of the *Lord who called you...*

Let me remind you... You are *NOT exempt* from His promises. We don't have the liberty to twist His words or pick when they do and don't apply.

He said, "If you love me, and if you follow me, I WILL use *all things* in your life for *good*." He said he has *more* in store than we can imagine. ...*Wow!*

Friend, I think you and I both ought to soak that in. *Believe it*. And keep walking in *faith*.

_____

Reflect: Are you working on something, and wondering if it's *worth* it? Do you believe God has so much *good* ahead as you keep following His lead? **(Write out your thoughts.)**

_____

_____

_____

_____

_____

_____

Pray: Lord God. Some days I hear you clearly and follow with ease, while others are confusing and I question if I'm on the *right* path. Lord, I know if I cling to *you*, you will *never* steer me wrong. And if I follow *your* lead faithfully, my journey will be paved with *more good* than I could imagine. Help me *hold tight* to that. Thank you for that. In your *perfect* name, Amen. **(Add your own personal prayer of praise, admission, and petition for today.)**

_____

_____

_____

_____

_____

_____

Seek The Word: Now to him who is able to do immeasurably more than all we ask or imagine, according to his power that is at work within us. (Ephesians 3:20) And we know that in all things God works for the good of those who love him, who have been called according to his purpose. (Romans 8:28) **(What speaks to you in the scripture? Note any other passages that come to mind.)**

_____

_____

_____

_____

_____

_____

What else is on your mind today? **Let your thoughts overflow below...**

_____

_____

_____

_____

_____

_____

_____

_____

_____

_____

_____

_____

_____

_____

_____

_____

_____

_____

_____

_____

_____

Peace, joy, energy... goodness. Oh how I want to be *overflowing* with these things. The entire human race is starved for such riches, *I see it.*

There's turmoil. In this world, in our families, relationships, and on social media - no doubt. It's so unsettling. *Isn't it?*

My rocky emotions finally tipped the boat into a sea of disheartenment last week. But I was determined not to sink. *You know why?* Because I've learned of a *good* God who *loves* me. *Each one of us* in fact, who will not let us fall if we *lean* on *him*.

Surely there's something that has *you* disheartened too? And first let me say... you are *not* alone. I feel you. My friend, I see you.

But now I want to remind you, like I need the DAILY reminder myself... If you lean harder, *rely more deeply*, on *God*, He will *rescue* your drowning soul and carry you to dry land. Where His *peace*, His *strength*, and *joy* are waiting to greet you.

Go to Him. *Lean* on Him. *Rely...* on *Him*.

I promise you, *He* promises you...The more you lean into Him today, the more His *blessings will fill your way.*

Reflect: Are you needing a "pick me up?" Will you allow *God* to be your *"go to"* for *all* that you *need* today? **(Write out your thoughts.)**

_____

_____

_____

_____

_____

Pray: Dear Lord, I feel the pull down, out, and all over. I want to be filled with your peace and *all* the goodness you have to offer. Help me lean harder on you today so that I may receive what you have your arms open to so freely give. In your *great* name I pray, Amen. **(Add your own personal prayer of praise, admission, and petition for today.)**

_____

_____

_____

_____

_____

_____

Seek the Word: Seek the LORD and his strength; seek his presence continually! (1 Chronicles 16:11) And this same God who takes care of me will supply all your needs from his glorious riches, which have been given to us in Christ Jesus. (Philippians 4:19) **(What speaks to**

you in the scripture? Note any other passages that come to mind.)

_____

_____

_____

_____

_____

_____

_____

_____

_____

_____

_____

_____

_____

_____

_____

_____

_____

_____

_____

_____

_____

What else is on your mind today? **Let your thoughts overflow below...**

_____

_____

_____

_____

_____

_____

_____

_____

_____

_____

_____

_____

_____

_____

_____

_____

_____

_____

Shame on me.

As I stumbled to the bathroom to wipe the sleep from my eyes, I allowed the simmer of grumbling to slip into my wearied morning fog.

I know better by now. The life of joy and peace I've been running hard after has no space for complaints and victimizing thoughts of self-pity. But, when I settle my gaze on what seems wrong, the reality of all that's good, is hidden in the shadows.

We do it to ourselves. *And I began to.* But... I fought back.

You know you have a choice to shift too? God *in* us is a bajillion times stronger than the enemy, and anything the world wants to throw us off course with. I rested my face in the palms of my hands, lowered my head before the Lord, and asked Him to show me what *HE* sees.

I closed my eyes, resisting the enemy's temptation to feed the overwhelm and exhaust of the "busy hangover" from the day past... my teenage son's social, sport, and work "running's around," the volleyball tournament town-hop back and forth with my 12-year-old daughter, the wee hours of the night sleepover with my 5th grader and a new friend, in tow with or our two strong-willed toddlers who are quick to escalate any craze. *I'm sure you can rehash some recent wild days too, yes?*

But, in this shift of focus, *instead* of wallowing in the ache of my waning energy... *I chose to praise God.* I peered through the filter of his perfect love and goodness, and thanked Him for children with a desire for relationships and the opportunity of inclusion. For their physical ability to even play sports and the chance to see them beam with bonds building and life lessons looming.

I remembered a friend's sorrow shared of a child with *no* friends, one with a disable son, and another who'd lost a daughter tragically and would give their life to hear the symphony of twin voices nagging each other... And I praised God for the gift of simply *having* children. And for the breath in my lungs that morning to praise Him for *all of this*.

God has blessed us with so much, but Satan doesn't want us to see it. The enemy wants you sulking in busyness, dissatisfaction, and defeat. He wants to take what God intended to lift you up, and cause it to break you down.

The choice is yours. *Who's view will you choose?* Don't let Satan trick you into the self-pity pit.

Maybe you *do* need to rest for a sec if your plate is overflowing. But, use the pause to adjust your sight to HIS lens, and reflect on how *good our God is*, who lovingly allowed you *beautiful* things to *fill* your days.

Reflect: Do you feel worn down by your busyness? Or are you noticing more bad than good around you lately? **(Write out your thoughts.)**

_____

_____

_____

_____

_____

_____

_____

Pray: Lord Jesus, Life is full and I'm guilty of grumbling about the lack of perfection around me. Help me pause and breathe in gratitude for the very things that weigh me down that *you intended* to bless me. You are a good God full of infinite gifts. Thank you for your light in the midst of the shadows. In your loving name, Amen. **(Add your own personal prayer of praise, admission, and petition for today.)**

_____

_____

_____

_____

_____

_____

Seek the Word: You intended to harm me, but God intended it for good to accomplish what is now being done, the saving of many lives. (Genesis 50:20) Let all that I am praise the LORD; may I never forget the good things he does for me. (Psalm 103:2) **(What speaks to you in the scripture? Note any other passages that come to mind.)**

_____

_____

_____

_____

_____

What else is on your mind today? Let your thoughts overflow
below...

_____

_____

_____

_____

_____

_____

_____

_____

_____

_____

_____

_____

_____

_____

_____

_____

_____

_____

_____

_____

Do you ever wonder why you *struggle* so much? When others seem to roll through life's punches with ease.

Year after year I pondered this perplexing question about myself.

And when I started noticing it wasn't always necessarily that my *circumstances* were worse off than "hers," I then got caught up in the angst of something-must-really-be-wrong-with-me self reflections.

Why do I feel bummed when others are beaming with smiles of contentment? What's with my lingering worry when fellow believers radiate unshakable trust in whatever God plants in their path?

Was I missing something?

Well maybe I was. Maybe you are too, if you can relate to this nagging introspection.

But here's what I've learned. My struggle, your struggle, is a *gift*. Our **weakness is a gift.**

And noting that God uses all things for good, this certainly applies to the weakness he uniquely allowed *you* to wrestle with.

God uses our flaws and fragility to remind us how much *we need him*. So that we will rely harder on him, to make us stronger, to reveal his faithfulness... and so that we may ***encourage others*** who are feeling weak. (Yes, sometimes it's not even about you.)

So let's do that today...

Lean on him.

Find your *strength* in *him*.

Thank him for his *faithfulness*.

And go find someone to *love* and *encourage*.

Reflect: Do you ever feel weak and wonder *why*? Have you considered it may be a gift to later reveal something greater? Or to help *you*, "help" *someone*? **(Write out your thoughts.)**

\
\
\
\
\
\
\

Pray: Lord God, my weakness is a difficult companion. I long for what's simpler and smooth, but I know through my struggles you have gifted me a precious deeper need for *you*. Because of this, I am growing in intimacy with you, and I thank you for this *invaluable treasure*. Help me find strength in *you* and shine a light to others... for *your* sake. They need you, just as I did, *I do*, and I *always* will. In your protective name, Amen. **(Add your own personal prayer of praise, admission, and petition for today.)**

_____

_____

_____

_____

_____

_____

Seek the Word: But he said to me, "My grace is sufficient for you, for my power is made perfect in weakness." Therefore I will boast all the more gladly about my weaknesses, so that Christ's power may rest on me. (2 Corinthians 12:9) **(What speaks to you in the scripture? Note any other passages that come to mind.)**

_____

_____

_____

_____

_____

_____

_____

_____

What else is on your mind today? Let your thoughts overflow below...

_____

_____

_____

_____

_____

_____

_____

_____

_____

_____

_____

_____

_____

_____

_____

_____

_____

_____

_____

_____

Do you ever wonder what in the world you're doing?

As in, I have *no business*... Parading around in this position I am obviously unqualified for; sitting among a bunch of smarties in this over-my-head class; parenting kids who should've been gifted a mom with oodles of energy; hanging with friends maintaining way more togetherness than my mess-of-a-life; being a part of a family needing so much more than I have to dish out...

I have no business doing... (you fill in the blank). *Seriously!* Who do I think *I am?*

How about you? Ever feel like some sort of fraud in a situation you've wound up in? Where you almost feel misplaced, and truthfully *not good enough?*

Wake up call alert.

This is a lie you are believing.

You are good enough, with *immeasurable worth* as God's handy creation.

AND... God didn't allow you to be where you are for nothing. He placed *intentional* purpose in all he orchestrates and creates. *He loves you **like crazy**.* And whether it's to teach you, bless you, prepare you, or serve the heart of another one of his beloveds, he's got you in your position for *good reason.*

If he leads you there, he'll feed you there... With just what you need to get the job done. *His job done.* He wants you to take part in his beautiful story because he loves you ***that*** much.

He made you. He loves you. And He wants to *use* you.

Ask him today to show you how he wants to use *your* situation and *your* placement to help his light shine. He may very well eventually move you elsewhere with a new mission, but he wants to use you *right where you are*, right *now*, as well.

If you ask and seek, whatever you're enduring, God can bring joy *through it* to your life. Joy that will seep out as blessings you'll begin to take notice of... from the *very thing* you *thought* you weren't cut out for.

Reflect: Do you feel "not good enough" in a particular area of your life? Do you realize you are placed for a purpose? **(Write out your thoughts.)**

_____

_____

_____

_____

_____

_____

Pray: God, you created me, and your love for me is greater than I can imagine. You have plans to use me, to use *everything* in my path to fulfill your good purpose. Thank you for giving me all that I need and

allowing me to be part of your glory story. In your loving name, Amen.
**(Add your own personal prayer of praise, admission, and
petition for today.)**

_____

_____

_____

_____

_____

_____

_____

Seek the Word: May you experience the love of Christ, though it is
too great to understand fully. Then you will be made complete with all
the fullness of life and power that comes from God. (Ephesians 3:19)
No, in all these things we are more than conquerors through him who
loved us. (Romans 8:37) **(What speaks to you in the scripture?
Note any other passages that come to mind.)**

_____

_____

_____

_____

_____

_____

_____

What else is on your mind today? **Let your thoughts overflow below...**

_____

_____

_____

_____

_____

_____

_____

_____

_____

_____

_____

_____

_____

_____

_____

_____

_____

_____

_____

_____

You're not in control. God is. So, you can take it easy.

If these words were a song, it would surely be my number one repeated tune. I nag myself daily, sometimes hourly, with the reminder... that I am NOT the god of all my "goings-on" and I'm wasting loads of energy trying to assume this monstrous role.

Do you run yourself ragged too? With assertive attempts to do it ALL? Take care of everyone... *everything*... each demanding time sucking detail, and then some?

I bet you're convinced if you could simply handle this, finish that, or get on top of whatever else, you'd finally gain some composure, sense a bit of joy and relief, and get that R & R you've been longing for - once *and for all.*

And this is what the enemy wants. To see you running around NUTS on the notorious hamster wheel. You're working relentlessly and tirelessly in order to "take it easy" - at least I am most of the time - but the truth is, we can take it easy... NOW.

You might be A-OK running the show... BUT...if you're exhausted, if you're "spent" trying to carry too big of a load, would you just *STOP* with me for a minute? God doesn't want you to be miserable. Pause and *know* that He certainly will provide for you and all the things you're scurrying around trying to control.

It may seem supernatural to assume time and space can be shifted without our human hand on everything in front of us, but THAT is what God is. THAT is what He *does*. His power is greater than any human mind can fathom.

All you need to know is that He has a *good* plan, He is *fully* capable of caring for *all* things, and His will WILL be done. So if you're feeling weary in your fight for control, you can breathe in some peace and take it easy, sweet friend. Because the control does not and will *never* belong to you. He's got ALL things in HIS mighty good hands.

Reflect: Are you feeling weary? Are you assuming too much control of your physical or mental load? Could you benefit from easing up a little and allowing God to do His work? **(Write out your thoughts.)**

_____

_____

_____

_____

_____

_____

Pray: All powerful God, I admit, I neglect to remember You are in control of the details of my day. Help me lean more on You and less on myself, so that I may receive the refreshment You offer in Your almighty presence. I am gratefully blessed with Your intentional care of each aspect of my life. Thank you for Your constant protection and peace. In Your glorious name, Amen. **(Add your own personal prayer of praise, admission, and petition for today.)**

_____

_____

_____

_____

_____

_____

Seek The Word: The heart of man plans his way, but the Lord establishes his steps. (Proverbs 16:9) But Jesus looked at them and said, "With man this is impossible, but with God all things are possible." (Matthew 19:26) Many are the plans in the mind of a man, but it is the purpose of the Lord that will stand. (Proverbs 19:21) **(What speaks to you in the scripture? Note any other passages that come to mind.)**

_____

_____

_____

_____

_____

_____

_____

_____

_____

What else is on your mind today? Let your thoughts overflow below...

_____

_____

_____

_____

_____

_____

_____

_____

_____

_____

_____

_____

_____

_____

_____

_____

_____

_____

I did something I rarely do last week... *I asked for prayer.*

A *peace-less pit* is where I had found myself. In a trench of unanswered prayer filling fast with anxiousness and self-reliant striving to determine my own destiny. Stuffed on top of perpetual pride. Too proud to ask for help, and definitely too proud to ask for *prayer.*

My book proposal had been submitted to 18 publishers six weeks prior. The wait for a "yes," combined with the trickle in of now nine rejection letters, was taking its toll on my encouragement and the hope I had built up and borrowed.

Now, don't get me wrong, I would pray. In fact, I was pleading for *peace* every single morning. But, as soon as I reached my "Amen," the enemy slithered back by with whiffs of doubt and dismay, smothering the sweet scent of serenity.

It was as if *I needed reinforcement.* All hands on deck to open my complete surrender and reveal the provision and power of God's peace and comforting presence.

So I succumbed... and swallowed my pride. I asked others to join me in prayer for a "yes" in the coming week from a publisher, because encouragement was depleting while discouragement swelling. But more importantly, I noted my desperate desire for *peace* in the *pause* for God's answer.

I bet you can guess what happened... No, I didn't get the "yes" (keep praying), but I did get what I *needed...* I got PEACE. *Praise God!*

How about you? Chances are, you're praying for something too. Would you email me and share? I believe in prayer. *God does listen.* And He *answers.* I'd love to help strengthen your plea and voice before him.

And even if you don't get exactly what you're praying for, or in the time you'd like... Can you imagine how *saturating peace* washing over you might drastically change your days? Infusing light and bright to your darkened dragging *wait*?

Peace changes everything. *Prayer* opens the door to *peace.* And it can be *yours.* Try it. It might feel fleeting with quick abandon, but then pray some more. And ask others to join you.

And before you come up with an excuse as to why your *something* isn't significant enough to bother God, remember to never question the size of your request. If it matters to you, *it matters to Him.* Because (another reminder) he loves you *wildly.*

Pray... And linger in peace today, sweet friend.

Reflect: What have you been praying for? Have you continued to ask for peace while you wait? Have you asked others to pray for you? **(Write out your thoughts.)**

_____

_____

Pray: Lord God, you know my heart. You know my deepest desires and my current concerns. I need your peace. Fill me with your comforting presence and sturdy faith in your reliable faithfulness. In your abundant name, Amen. **(Add your own personal prayer of praise, admission, and petition for today.)**

_____

_____

_____

_____

_____

_____

Seek the Word: "...in every situation, by prayer and petition, with thanksgiving, present your requests to God. And the peace of God, which transcends all understanding, will guard your hearts and your minds in Christ Jesus." (Philippians 4:6b - 7) **(What speaks to you in the scripture? Note any other passages that come to mind.)**

_____

_____

_____

_____

What else is on your mind today? Let your thoughts overflow below...

_____

_____

_____

_____

_____

_____

_____

_____

_____

_____

_____

_____

_____

_____

_____

_____

_____

_____

_____

_____

Friend, it was my honor to journey with you through *Faith Fueled*!

If you enjoyed our walk together...

Would you consider

helping me FUEL the FAITH of others by leaving a

Review on Amazon?

**Scan this QR code to find the Amazon listing
& leave your review!**
Grab a copy for a friend to encourage in faith while you're at it! ;)

Then, subscribe to my future devotionals at KERI-ANN.COM
& come hang out with me on social so we can stay connected!

    @ K e r i A n n _ E i c h b e r g e r
    @ K e r i A n n E i c h b e r g e r
    @ K e r i A n n _ W r i t e r

Thank you! You are a Blessing! - Keri